Original title:
The Fruit That Grows

Copyright © 2025 Creative Arts Management OÜ
All rights reserved.

Author: Alec Davenport
ISBN HARDBACK: 978-1-80586-451-6
ISBN PAPERBACK: 978-1-80586-923-8

Tangled in Orchard Light

In the orchard, apples giggle,
Pears dance, making shadows wiggle.
Cherries chuckle in a swarm,
While blueberries plot a fruity charm.

Lemons jive with zesty flair,
Oranges toss their peels in air.
Grapes are bouncing, what a sight,
In this jolly, tangled light.

Banquet of Sun-Kissed Delights

Berries bask on a grand buffet,
With fruits in chaos, bright and gay.
Melons roll and grapes collide,
In this feast, they take great pride.

Bowls of laughter, colors bright,
Tasting joy, a pure delight.
Peaches whisper jokes so sweet,
While bananas break into a beat.

Blooming Under the Sun

Under the sun, the fruits conspire,
In their world, they'll never tire.
Fruits in colors, bright and bold,
Tell their secrets, pure and gold.

Pineapples wear hats of green,
While figs play hide and seek unseen.
Limes roll laughter down the lane,
Their fruity puns will drive you insane!

Curves of Nature's Palette

With curves and shapes that twist and sway,
Fruits have fun in a charming way.
Apples, round like summer's smile,
Mangoes laugh, they go the extra mile.

Coconuts drop with a playful thud,
Raspberries giggle, spilling their blood.
Nature's palette, wild and free,
In this garden, joy's the key!

Nature's Sweet Mosaic

In gardens wild, they tumble down,
Bananas wear a silly frown.
Apples giggle with each bite,
While pears dance in the warm daylight.

Cherries play a game of tag,
Lemons laugh, a sunny brag.
Kiwi whispers, green and bright,
Melons roll with pure delight.

Blossoms of Tomorrow

Buds that burst with daring flair,
Citrus smells fill up the air.
Plum trees chat with breezy zest,
As grapes play cards, forgetting rest.

Peaches blush, a cheeky sight,
While nectarines slide left and right.
Raspberries giggle, tangled tight,
Their juice spills out - oh what a fright!

Seeds of Summer Dreams

Seeds of futures, silly schemes,
Sprout from soil, like quirky dreams.
Watermelons wear straw hats,
While avocados chat with bats.

Coconuts begin to sway,
Pretending they can dance and play.
Mangoes prance in sunny lanes,
While under them, a chicken complains.

The Language of Ripening

Plump tomatoes pull a prank,
Sneaky cucumbers join the prank.
Squash giggles, round and true,
While peppers play alongside the crew.

Berries blush under the warm sun,
Whispering secrets, having fun.
Each ripe laugh, a joyful sound,
In this garden playground found.

Echoes of the Garden's Heart

In the garden where giggles sprout,
Tomatoes dance and peas jump about.
Strawberries sing their sweet little tune,
While carrots are plotting a vegetable heist at noon.

Rabbits wear shades, act like a star,
Peeking at veggies from the back of a car.
Comedic chaos beneath the sun's glow,
Laughter abounds where the greenies grow.

The Dance of Roots and Canopy

Roots are wiggling, trying to groove,
While leaves above sway, showing their move.
A cabbage cracks jokes with a cheeky sprout,
The soil below is where the fun's about.

Beneath the earth, worms giggle in soil,
While radishes plan a grand veggie toil.
Sunflowers sway like they're on a spree,
What a sight, a leafy jubilee!

Juicy Tales of the Earth

Once, a peach played hide and seek,
With a foot in the sun, and a cheek so meek.
Cherries chuckled as lemons threw pies,
Oh, the laughter beneath sunny skies!

Raspberries tell wild tales of the days,
When they raced each other in berry-filled ways.
A coconut spins like a dancer in shorts,
While limes crack wise 'bout their citrusy ports.

Murmurs of the Harvest Moon

Under the moon, squash start a band,
With pumpkins as drums, oh, isn't it grand?
Zucchini strums on a twig made from vines,
As apples and pears tell silly punchlines.

Fallen leaves do a tango in flight,
While grapes have a party, oh what a sight!
As the night hums, and joy takes its flight,
The harvest moon grins at the festive delight.

Invoking Nature's Richness

In a garden where laughter blooms,
Tomatoes dance in their leafy rooms.
Carrots wear hats, quite bold and bright,
While peas tell jokes under the moonlight.

Bananas giggle as they peel away,
Radishes roll in a playful fray.
Nature's buffet, a riot of cheer,
With veggies and fruits that bring us near.

The Language of Sweetness

Citrus skits with zesty flair,
Bananas slip but don't much care.
Kiwis whisper secrets sweet,
While melons toss their seeds like feet.

Pineapples wear crowns, they boast and show,
As strawberries twirl in a berry glow.
Caught in a comedy of flavors so fine,
Every bite's a punchline, that's our line!

In the Shadow of Seasons

Fall brings apples, plump and round,
While pumpkins roll on the autumn ground.
Cherries chuckle in the spring breeze,
As the flowers bloom with laughter and tease.

Summer's corn pops with joy, quite loud,
While grapes sip sun in a giggly crowd.
Nature's cycle is a playful game,
Where every season earns its fame.

Fruitful Reveries

Avocados posing, green and slick,
Comparing outfits, what a trick!
Lemons frown with their sour pout,
But we all know they're sweet inside out.

Pears lounge like kings in their sunny space,
Ripe peaches giggle, oh what a race!
Dancing to rhythms of the breeze above,
These playful treats are filled with love.

Drumbeats of Growing Green

In the garden, a dance begins,
Wiggly worms join in the spins.
Tomatoes giggle, peppers cheer,
While carrots tug at roots held dear.

Radishes poke their little heads,
Singing songs from cozy beds.
Pumpkins puff with splendid pride,
Wishing to take a joyride!

Harvest Time Whispers

The cornfields buzz with little bees,
Whispering secrets on the breeze.
Apples laugh as they fall down low,
Making cider, don't you know?

Berries flirt with every passerby,
Wanting all to stop and try.
A pie made here, a tart made there,
Baking treats with tasty flair!

As Seasons Rotate

Spring brings blooms with sassy flair,
Blossoms waving, saying, "No fair!"
Summer's heat makes everyone sweat,
Cucumbers laughing like a pet.

Autumn's leaves in colors bright,
Fruits blushing with delight.
Winter hides the seeds away,
Dreaming of the sunny day.

The Hidden Gold of Nature

Beneath the soil, a treasure sleeps,
Believing dreams that nature keeps.
Mischievous onions shed their skin,
While potatoes giggle where they've been.

Golden squash with a cheeky grin,
Flaunts its curves, let's all dig in!
Hidden gems beneath the ground,
In laughter and joy, they abound!

Blossoms in the Afternoon

In a garden of chaos, bees buzz wide,
Petals flutter, a floral tide.
Giggles from tomatoes, ripe and round,
A cucumber learns to dance, profound.

Sunshine drips from every vine,
Pumpkins plotting a comedic line.
Butterflies wear hats, fancy and bright,
While carrots giggle at their silly plight.

The Dance of Orchard Spirits

Orchards twirl in a leafy trance,
Fruits all join in a merry dance.
Apples try their hand at a jig,
While grapes roll around, oh so big!

Peaches have flair, they shimmy and sway,
Though plums prefer to nap all day.
Cherries burst out in raucous song,
"Join us, come on, you can't go wrong!"

Of Ripe Pears and Gentle Breezes

Pears in line, looking quite round,
Whispering secrets without a sound.
A breeze sneaks in with a playful tease,
Making tangerines giggle with ease.

Lemons squirt laughter, sour and sweet,
As limes dance circles, quick on their feet.
"Is it just me?" says a peach with glee,
"We might just be the best fruit, you'll see!"

Savoring the Season's Gifts

Basket full of wonders, each one a treat,
Zucchini's got jokes, isn't that neat?
Radishes chuckle, their tops in dismay,
"Who knew we'd be the stars today?"

Cherries play tag, it's a riot for sure,
Blueberries cheer, "We're small but pure!"
Strawberries wink, going all out,
"This fruity party's what it's about!"

Symbol of Renewal

In a garden where laughter blooms,
Cucumbers wear hats, making rooms.
Strawberries dance in polka dots,
Winking at bees and all that it spots.

Tomatoes toss their seeds in glee,
Cabbage sings a song, so carefree.
Carrots grin, all tangled and spry,
Swaying to rainclouds passing by.

Bananas peel in comedic style,
Zucchini jokes, but with a smile.
Here's a place where veggies play,
In the sunlit joy of the day.

So let's plant seeds of mischief, too,
In this patch where giggles grew.
Fertilize with funny banter,
And watch as nature's jesters canter.

Garden of Wishes and Whimsy

In a patch of dreams and silly schemes,
Radishes roam in moonlit beams.
Pumpkins wear glasses, wise and bold,
While beans tell stories from the old.

Once a carrot dressed in green,
Claimed he was a regal machine.
He ruled the rows with veggie cheer,
While lettuce laughed, "Don't you dare steer!"

Tomatoes hid in playful fright,
Seeking shadows from the light.
The peas plotted a fun escape,
Dreaming of a veggie grape cape.

In this garden where laughter spritz,
Even beets do the waltz with glitz.
A place where wishes sprout and twirl,
In the land of whimsy, they unfurl.

Pathways to Aromatic Abundance

In the aisles of herb-scented fun,
Thyme and rosemary sing as one.
Basil twirls in a fragrant dance,
Oregano catches a garlic glance.

Chives play tag with parsley's grace,
While dill starts a flower face race.
Mint grows wild, in laughter's grip,
Tickling noses with its fresh quip.

This walkway's paved with zesty cheer,
Spices giggle, it's clear, oh dear!
The sage does yoga, calm and spry,
While cloves whisper secrets, passing by.

Join this parade of tasty delight,
Where every plant shines bright and light.
In the realm of scents, we parade,
With giggles and flavors, unafraid.

Seasons of Flavor and Hope

In a world where flavors collide,
Summer fruits giggle, cheeks full of pride.
Apples wear pajamas, all cozy at night,
While oranges juggle, what a sight!

Spring bursts forth with peas on high,
Raspberries hover like clouds in the sky.
Cabbages gossip, what can they tell?
As beets boast loudly, "We taste so swell!"

Autumn arrives with a crunching sound,
Pumpkins play hopscotch on the ground.
Fall leaves flutter, sporting golden hats,
While squirrels share muffins with chubby chats.

Winter wraps all in a frosty gig,
Carrots in snow have a silly jig.
In every season, there's laughter and cheer,
With flavors of hope that'll always endear.

The Orchard's Secret Symphony

In orchards where the laughter waits,
The apples dance on wobbly plates.
Pears juggle as the squirrels cheer,
While lemons sing, we all appear.

A chorus of leaves rustles on high,
With grapes that giggle as they fly.
The cherries blush with every joke,
As playful winds begin to poke.

Bees buzz along in a buzzing hum,
While pumpkins roll and boast of fun.
Ripe berries tossed in a game of catch,
Join the symphony; there's no match!

So grab a basket, come and play,
In this wild grove where we laugh all day.
Nature's concert where all can sway,
Join the rhythm, come what may!

Time's Palette of Sweetness

Brushes dipped in colors bright,
A canvas where each bite's a delight.
The oranges wink, with zest so bold,
While bananas slip, their magic unfolds.

Strawberries wear their seeds like crowns,
As peaches roll through leafy towns.
Figs laugh in their paper dress,
Making every moment a sweet mess.

Ripe raspberries racing through the vines,
Cherries plotting their heist of pines.
Every fruit has a story told,
In this colorful orchard, joy unfolds.

So taste the hues of every treat,
In this palette, life's bittersweet.
Work of art on every tree,
A flavor explosion, wild and free!

From Seed to Sun

It starts with a seed, so tiny and meek,
Dreaming of growth, adventure to seek.
With dirt as their bed, and sunshine their friend,
They reach for the sky, on joy they depend.

Sprouts peek out with a curious grin,
Waving hello to the world, let's begin!
Leaves tickling each other as they unfurl,
In this playful dance, watch nature swirl.

Growing up strong, they giggle in rows,
While winds carry whispers of how it all goes.
Branches weave tales of how trees might kiss,
In this garden of joy, nothing's amiss.

Now ripe and ready, they're ripe for a quest,
Messy and sweet, oh, they're truly blessed.
From seed to sun, with laughter bestowed,
Nature's adventure is a funny episode!

Hummingbird's Feast

A hummingbird zips, all speedy and spry,
Dancing in flowers, oh my, oh my!
Nectar so sweet, it's quite the treat,
A sugar rush dance on tiny feet.

With a twist and a twirl, it flitters about,
As blossoms giggle, there's no doubt.
Colors collide like a carnival fight,
In this vibrant banquet, everything's right.

The blooms all gossip, sharing their tales,
Of nectar quests and windy gales.
The bird just laughs, sips up the fun,
Under the bright and shining sun.

So as the feast continues to swirl,
Nature's ballet makes the heart twirl.
Join the party, don't miss the crunch,
Where the hummingbird feasts, and laughter is lunch!

Brimming with Life's Elixir

In the orchard, giggles burst,
Apples dance, a juicy thirst.
Oranges juggling, what a sight,
Lemons laughing, pure delight.

Peaches play their fuzzy game,
Bananas slip; who's to blame?
Cherries chirp and laugh a song,
In this grove where we belong.

Mangoes swing from branches high,
Strawberries wave as we pass by.
Fruits of humor hanging there,
In this laughter-laden air.

So grab a pear and take a bite,
Let your worries take a flight.
Savor sweetness, feel the cheer,
In this colorful atmosphere.

Solar Cruise

On a sunny boat, we float with grace,
Melons round the hull, taking space.
Kiwis wearing shades, sipping juice,
Pineapples dancing, let them loose!

Grapes are jammin' to a beat,
Ripe and plump, they can't be beat.
Chillin' hard on boards so fine,
Fruits together in a line.

Coconuts take charge the helm,
While lemons guard their fruity realm.
Avocados make the coolest crew,
Navigating waves, a fruity view.

So raise a toast to this sweet ride,
With fruity friends all by our side.
In the sun, we glide and spin,
Life's a cruise, let's dive right in!

Of Vine and Sky

On trellises, each grape's a star,
Stretching vines that reach afar.
Berries blush with rosy glee,
Hanging out, wild and free.

Tomatoes sport their vibrant hue,
Chasing shadows, seeking dew.
Raspberries giggle in the breeze,
Tickling leaves and bumblebees.

Old pumpkins whisper tales of yore,
While zucchinis plot to score.
Swaying softly, peas just grin,
In this garden where dreams begin.

Nature's crew, they play all day,
Mixing laughter in their sway.
Each vine a tale, each leaf a jest,
In the heart of play, we're truly blessed.

Sunkissed Horizons

Under skies of sparkling blue,
Fruits compete in a playful hue.
Watermelons laughing, oh so bold,
While cantaloupes tell tales of old.

Blueberries race, a fruity dash,
Ripe bananas in a giggling splash.
Papayas roll in joy and fun,
Sunkissed brains put on the run.

With sun above and roots below,
Fruity friends steal the show.
Life's a canvas, bright and free,
In nature's theater, we agree.

So join this merry fruity tale,
Raise your glass, let's set the sail.
To horizons kissed by golden rays,
In this fruity dance, we'll always play!

A Tapestry of Harvest Colors

In orchards bright with hues so wild,
The pumpkins grin like a cheeky child.
Each gourd in sight wears a funny face,
While cornstalks giggle in their place.

The apples wear hats, all shiny and round,
Their laughter echoes across the ground.
Bananas slip, trying not to trip,
As wind whispers secrets with a playful zip.

Sunflowers laugh as they dance in the breeze,
While grapes gossip high above the trees.
With every gust, the colors play,
Creating joy in the bright bouquet.

So come and join this harvest cheer,
Where nature's whimsy makes it clear.
A tapestry wove with laughter and fun,
In fields that sparkle beneath the sun.

Apples Afire with Autumn's Glow

In orchards bursting with cheerful schemes,
The apples blush with adventurous dreams.
They play hide and seek with the golden rays,
Hoping the sun is perfectly amazed.

They wear their skins of red and gold,
While squirrels chatter, all brave and bold.
A worm peeks out, quite the jest,
Claiming that apples are his best fest.

Each bite reveals a crisp delight,
With funny faces in every bite.
The crunch and squish, a joyful song,
In a world where everything feels right and wrong.

So gather round, let laughter ring,
As autumn's dance begins to swing.
With apples afire, bright in our view,
The orchard's a circus, just for you!

Beneath the Canopy of Abundance

Under leafy roofs where mischief dwells,
The fruits tell tales and weave their spells.
Beneath the canopy, giggles will sprout,
As cherries swing and give a shout.

Bananas hang low, with smiles askew,
In a bright yellow costume, just for you.
They slip on the ground, a giggle parade,
In this funny orchard, joy won't fade.

Peaches blush as the laughter grows,
They blush from laughter, who really knows?
The figs in the vines are having a ball,
While jolly blueberries try not to fall.

So join the feast, come share the glee,
In this bountiful world, wild and free.
Beneath the canopy, let joy pour,
With fruits having fun and wanting more!

Melon Mischief and Sunshine

In fields where melons roll and play,
They bounce and giggle throughout the day.
Watermelons wear sunglasses with flair,
While cantaloupes spin on the fresh air.

The vine whispers jokes with a twisty grin,
As juicy laughter bursts from within.
Honeydews chuckle, sharing their tales,
While pumpkin belly flops in the gales.

The sun beams down, quite a sight,
As melons laugh in pure delight.
With every slice, a party's unrolled,
In this funny garden, brave and bold.

So gather your friends, let the fun begin,
As we celebrate the juicy win.
Melon mischief under the sun so bright,
In a world where laughter feels just right.

Blooming Journeys

In a garden where laughter flies,
Bumblebees wear tiny ties.
They dance on blooms, so bright and bold,
Whispering secrets of nectar untold.

A tomato dreams of being red,
While carrots brag about what they've bred.
The radish rolls its eyes in glee,
'I'm kickin' it with parsley and me!'

Sunflowers try a stand-up joke,
But the cucumbers just choke and soak.
Lettuce laughs with leafy flair,
As squash gets tangled in its hair.

So come and join this comic tease,
Where every plant is sure to please.
The garden's full of silly sights,
With chuckles bouncing from day to night.

Tasting The Sweetness of Dawn

Morning light on oranges gleams,
As lemons plot their citrus dreams.
Cherries giggle, hanging tight,
While grapefruits argue over height.

Peaches pose, all fuzzy and fine,
Claiming they are truly divine.
A banana slips with a grin,
Saying, 'I'm just ripe for a win!'

Raspberries blush, all too aware,
Of how they lead the berry affair.
They throw a party, oh what fun,
With jam and jelly on the run.

Every bite is like a song,
Juicy laughter where we belong.
With tangy twists and fruity puns,
A morning feast that never shuns.

In the Heart of the Grove

In the grove, all fruits convene,
With cheeky jokes and sights unseen.
Avocados wear their best green coats,
While pears are busy counting votes.

Lemons scribble rhymes with zest,
Claiming they can simply jest.
Figs laugh out loud, not shy at all,
Making puns that make us fall.

The apple's charm is quite the show,
While plums argue about their grow.
They swing like kids on branches high,
In the sunny, silly sky.

Bananas gossip, always bright,
As kiwi throws a quirky kite.
Here, every moment's pure delight,
In fruity fun, both day and night.

The Secret Lives of Fragrant Vines

Vines whisper secrets in the breeze,
Their leafy laughter brings us ease.
They twirl and dance in shades of green,
Creating mischief, quite the scene.

Grapes tease each other, snug and round,
Playing hide-and-seek on the ground.
While cucumbers, in their mellow bliss,
Attempt to steal a juicy kiss.

Pumpkins declare they're the best of all,
But all the squash have a ball.
They roll and tumble, full of cheer,
Spreading giggles far and near.

The garden's gossip's wild and ripe,
With every vine a different type.
So join the fun, let laughter flow,
In this secret place, where we all grow.

Harvest of Colors

In the orchard where colors blend,
Red and yellow, my taste buds fend.
Grapes doing yoga on twisted vines,
Apples giggle, sharing punchlines.

Bananas swing in a trendy dance,
Lemons squirt juice, a zesty chance.
Pears are gossiping, oh what a scene,
Fruits in costumes, a harvest dream!

Cherries play hide-and-seek on the tree,
While plums chant songs, oh so carefree.
Berries burst with mischief and cheer,
A carnival spreading bright smiles here!

As the sun dips low, the laughter grows,
A fruit fiesta, where fun overflows.
In this garden of giggles, we all partake,
Planting joy with every shake!

Eden's Silent Bounty

In a garden where secrets lie,
Lemons plot mischief, oh my, oh my!
Peaches wear hats and sip on tea,
While tomatoes converse about life's spree.

Carrots dream of becoming stars,
As cucumbers chatter about shiny cars.
Radishes compete with their spicy wit,
Telling tales of the fruits that don't fit.

Avocados pose, all dressed in green,
Strutting like models, if you know what I mean.
Grapefruit giggles, a citrus delight,
Planning a party on a warm summer night.

Everybody laughs, nobody's shy,
In this silent bounty where the fruits fly high.
A whimsical world, oh what a scene,
Where every bite says, "Life's a dream!"

Whispers Among the Vines

Beneath the leafy canopy, secrets spill,
Vines are gossiping, oh what a thrill!
Cucumbers overhear the humorous fuss,
While zucchinis roll, like they don't care much.

Pumpkins plotting their Halloween dreams,
Kale making smoothies with fruity beams.
Berries whisper sweet nothings so shy,
Plucking rhymes as butterflies fly by.

The onions giggle, shedding a tear,
As peas joke about what they might wear.
Radical radishes throwing a bash,
While sweet corn claps in a colorful flash.

Amidst the chaos, surprising delight,
Every vine humming songs of the night.
Oh, what a racket in this leafy maze,
Nature's own circus, a delightful craze!

Orchard's Embrace

In orchards filled with quirky charms,
Fruits embrace life with open arms.
Berries bounce on a trampoline,
Kiwis make smoothies, team up with beans.

Limes wear jackets that sparkle and shine,
Oranges dance, feeling oh so fine.
Bananas slip and slide with a grin,
What a wild party; let the fun begin!

Fruits in a frenzy, all in a row,
Peaches high-fiving as the wind starts to blow.
Pineapples wear crowns, looking so grand,
While cherries giggle, hand in hand.

The sun sets low; it's the end of the show,
But the laughter lingers everywhere we go.
In this orchard's embrace, joy knows no bounds,
Where whimsy and sweetness together resound!

Blossoms on the Wind

Petals dancing high in the air,
A bee in a tux, quite debonair.
Swirling like confetti, they zoom and spin,
Laughing as they tease the chubby kin.

Tiny buds whisper secrets so sweet,
To branches that wiggle their leafy feet.
A flower with socks, so silly and bright,
Sways with a giggle beneath the moonlight.

Breeze carries scents, a candy parade,
While fruit bats play charades in the shade.
They hang upside down, wearing silly grins,
Singing loud praises to their juicy twins.

So come take a look at this floral affair,
Where laughter grows wild, and none seem to care.
Life's a fruit bowl, all colors and cheer,
With each wacky blossom, the giggles draw near.

Roots in the Rich Earth

Under the surface, a root party's on,
With radishes dancing until the dawn.
Carrots don party hats made of green,
While worms groove to the earthworm machine.

A beet rolls in, doing the twist,
"Join our polka!" it can't resist.
Soils mix up in a muddy embrace,
While clumps of grass show off their best face.

"Oh look, it's a turnip!" they all shout,
With leaves like a crown, they laugh and pout.
The tubers unite in a hilarious jest,
Root camaraderie is simply the best.

And so they burrow, never a care,
Making the ground their stage to share.
When the world's above is wild and loud,
Just peek below—it's a veggie crowd!

Ripe Reflections

In the orchard, a mirror reflects a pear,
Winking at a peach with a fluffy hair.
'What a show!' says the cherry in red,
As the apple rolls by, cool in its spread.

"Did you hear the joke of the lemon?" it beams,
Sour-faced but giggling, bursting with dreams.
Berries chuckle, grouped in a mess,
A blissful bouquet in colorful dress.

Melons play tag, slipping and sliding,
Water on board, with laughter colliding.
Tropical rhythms sweep through the vines,
Creating a symphony as sweet as the wines.

In this garden of joy, every fruit has a role,
With laughter and fun, filling each bowl.
They savor their silliness, juicy and bright,
In a dance of reflections, pure delight.

The Taste of Twilight

As the sun dips low, snacks start to peek,
A grape in sunglasses, feeling unique.
With a sun-kissed complexion, the figs assemble,
Telling tales of summer as shadows tremble.

Plums prance forth on a narrow line,
"Who can skip stones? It's our time to shine!"
They giggle and tumble, quick as a flash,
As the evening unfolds, in a vibrant splash.

A kiwi with flair dons a top hat so grand,
While the oranges cheer from a tasty band.
"Let's toast to the moon!" a melon declares,
With joyful juice dribbling everywhere.

In this twilight, laughter fills the air,
With every sweet moment, they have their share.
Nature's delight, served fresh from the vine,
Where humor and sweetness forever entwine.

The Juicy Chronicles of Spring

In the garden, something's ripe,
Tomatoes wearing silly hype.
Carrots dance with leafy hands,
As radishes form rock 'n' bands.

Bees buzz in a goofy trance,
Pollinating plants that prance.
Peas giggle in their green coats,
While lettuce spins in twirly floats.

Strawberries wear a smile so bright,
Competing with the sun for light.
But cucumbers with their cool shades,
Are thinking of some summer parades.

In this garden, every sprout,
Has a silly song to shout.
As springtime brings its joyful cheer,
The veggies laugh, let's all draw near!

Petals Like Confetti in the Wind

Petals flutter, making noise,
Like playful little girls and boys.
Daisies giggle, they can't stay,
As butterflies join in the play.

Sunflowers wear their tallest hats,
Swinging with the chattering cats.
Tulips dance the hula line,
While violets sip on sweet sunshine.

Breezes blow, like whispers sweet,
Tickling every hopping beet.
The market's filled with fruity cheer,
As laughter fills the midair near.

In this floral, funny spree,
Nature's laughing joyfully.
With petals flying everywhere,
Life's confetti is a cheerful flair!

A Symphony of Citrus

Lemons jive in flashy zest,
While oranges hold a citrus fest.
Limes stir up a tangy rhyme,
In this party, they're in prime.

Grapefruits flip like acrobats,
Some roll around like playful cats.
Citrus scents create a tune,
As night creeps in beneath the moon.

Pineapples wear their prickly crowns,
And coconut shakes off its frowns.
With every squeeze, a giggle spills,
As peachy laughter fills the hills.

Orchestras of juicy delight,
Play music sweet, both day and night.
In this garden full of cheer,
Citrus fun is always near!

The Song of Sinking Sun on Grapes

Grapes are singing as day departs,
Their voices bubbling like fine arts.
Twilight whispers in purple hue,
While shadows dance where laughter grew.

The sun dips low, with golden rays,
Grapes giggle in the sunset haze.
Waltzing gently with the breeze,
As birds chirp tunes that aim to please.

Vines entwine in silly knots,
Tickling the soil with their thoughts.
In this vineyard, joy's the prize,
As grape jelly dreams illuminate the skies.

So raise a toast to evening's bliss,
With fruity tunes you won't want to miss.
As nighttime hums its quirky song,
The grape party's where we all belong!

Serene Cherries Beneath the Sun

In the garden, oh so bright,
Cherries hide from morning light.
A squirrel snoozes in the shade,
Dreaming of the pies he made.

Bouncing blobs in red attire,
Tickling branches, they conspire.
With every creak, the laughter swells,
As bees break out with silly yells.

They chatter, dance on stems so short,
While ants form lines for fruity sport.
If cherries giggle, who could blame?
Their juicy laughter, quite the fame!

So if you find a cherry grin,
Just know that mischief's deep within.
A fruity joke on sunny days,
Their silly ways leave us amazed.

Citrus Dreams Amongst Starlit Skies

Lemons argue 'bout the zest,
While oranges just laugh their best.
A grapefruit grumbles, what a fuss,
Claiming juiciness's a must!

At night, they shimmer, yellow glow,
Dancing shadows, putting on a show.
Cola clouds float all around,
As tangy tunes can be found.

Limes are lime-ing in their dreams,
With piñas swaying in moonbeams.
The stars take bites with citrus spark,
Creating laughter in the dark.

A cosmic fruit bowl in the sky,
Witty banter as they fly.
If you see them, don't be shy,
Join the fun and reach up high!

Orchard Lullabies

In the orchard, soft and sweet,
Apples whisper as we meet.
Crickets play a tune so soft,
While pears sway, their laughter loft.

A peach yells out, "I'm rocking this!"
While apricots give hugs with bliss.
A humble plum just rolls its eyes,
Snickers echo through the skies.

Underneath a leafy dome,
Each fruit dreams of its own home.
Treetops creak with stories bold,
Of secret games and treasures told.

As twilight dips into a song,
Fruity dreams where we belong.
So rest your head, do not think twice,
Join the lullabies, oh how nice!

The Splendor of Summer's Orchard

Summer rolls with juicy thrills,
And watermelons hide their chills.
A berry bounces, blissfully bright,
With seeds that giggle at the sight.

Plump tomatoes wear a crown,
Strut around, refusing a frown.
While radishes play peekaboo,
Tickling roots, oh, what a view!

Sunflowers sway to a fruity beat,
As the juiciest treats take a seat.
When moonlight spills its glowing grin,
The orchard crew starts to spin.

So join the party, feast your eyes,
In this harvest where laughter flies.
With every crunch and juicy bite,
Summer's orchard, pure delight!

Berry Wild Beneath the Stars

In the garden at night, oh what a sight,
Berries gleam like jewels, sparkling and bright.
Raspberries argue, 'I'm redder than you!'
While blueberries giggle, 'Oh, please, I'm the true!'

A strawberry claimed it could dance like a pro,
But tripped on a vine, took a tumble, oh no!
Cherries just laughed, hanging high with delight,
Synchronized swinging, they twinkled in flight.

Under the moon, they jest and they tease,
Bananas slip in, trying hard to appease.
But all join the chorus, a raucous affair,
These fruits in a frolic, a wild fruit fair!

And just when you think that the fun must all end,
The cucumbers chime in, 'Now, here we extend!'
They groove with a shuffle, and the nuts join the beat,
In this berry wild garden, there's never defeat!

Garden of Forgotten Flavors

In a garden lost, where flavors collide,
Pineapples waltz, but the leeks try to hide.
Radishes chuckle that they're far too sharp,
While veggies chat loudly, belting a harp.

The cabbage, a sage, tries to craft a new joke,
But all that it does is just make the folks choke!
Grapes roll their eyes and throw puns all around,
While onions just weep, their tears hit the ground.

A pumpkin player strums in the corner so bright,
His band of zucchinis are a lively delight.
They cover old songs of lemon and lime,
With a twist of the beet, oh what a good time!

Amongst all these flavors, with laughter that flies,
The radishes' raucous, a humorous surprise.
In this garden of taste, you'll find joy even rare,
With roots that are witty, beyond compare!

Luscious Tales of Tangy Bliss

In the grove where fruits chatter, what a delight,
Peaches tell stories that stretch through the night.
Plums roll their eyes while oranges puff up,
Saying, 'We're zesty, no need to erupt!'

Kiwi's ridiculous, with fuzzy green hair,
Claims that he's royal, just basking in flair.
Mangoes join in, with tales full of zest,
While bananas just crack up, thinking they're best.

Cranberries boast, 'We make holiday pies!'
But apples just snicker, 'Oh, what a surprise!'
With laughter audacious, fruit breaks into song,
A symphony sweet, where they all dance along.

And under the sun, as they twirl and they spin,
The world becomes joyful, so where to begin?
In tales spun of laughter, giggles in bliss,
Life's a luscious tale, you can't help but kiss!

Echoes of Flavorful Dreams

In a realm of pure flavor, where dreams take their flight,
Fruits whisper secrets in the shimmering light.
Watermelons ponder who tastes best on cake,
While lemons just croon, 'We'll make your heart ache!'

Blueberries joke that they're royalty grand,
While cantaloupe jests that it's hard to withstand.
Tangerines giggle, 'We're citrus divine!'
As raspberries roll off, 'Nah, we're truly fine!'

Pomegranates boast of their juicy delight,
While cherries just pop, oh what a sweet sight!
Lucious tales echo, enticing our dreams,
In this zany fruit world, nothing's as it seems.

From the stems of the trees to the ground they do fall,
These echoes of laughter are the heart of it all.
So gather your friends, in this flavorful scene,
For the dreams that we share are the best ever seen!

Seasons Wrapped in Green

In springtime's humor, blooms appear,
They tickle the noses, bring smiles and cheer.
A pear tree winks, its branches sway,
"I've got more pears than you can sway!"

In summer's warmth, the laughter's loud,
Cherries giggle, drawing quite a crowd.
They throw raucous parties, juicy and fine,
While plums bust out, claiming they'll shine.

As autumn's breeze begins to play,
The apples jest, "We're here to stay!"
They dress in gold, then slip and fall,
Landing with splats, oh what a call!

Then winter arrives, with a cozy grin,
Berries tell stories, of summer's win.
"We'll brew you tea, make you feel nice,
With a sprinkle of laughter and just a slice!"

Sunlit Cradles of Joy

In a sunny patch, tomatoes lounge,
They flex their skins, make the neighbors frown.
"Hey there cucumber, you think you're slick?"
"Just wait till salad, I'll give you a kick!"

Zucchini's dressed in stripes so bold,
"I'm not a vegetable, I'm worth my gold!"
A squash retorts, with a cheeky smirk,
"In this garden race, I'm such a perk!"

Bees buzz along, with a honeyed laugh,
They tease the blooms, "We're doing the math!"
Pollen is gold, that's the buzz of the day,
Adding sweet giggles in a busy ballet!

As dusk falls down, fireflies twirl,
"Catch me if you can, come on, give it a whirl!"
The veggies sigh, smile, and sway,
As moonlight whispers, "Let's dance, hooray!"

Melodies of the Bursting Orchard

In orchards wide, a symphony plays,
Where pears and apples jive in the rays.
A berry chorus sings, "We're so full of zest!"
While peaches parade in puffy best!

Cider's on deck, saying, "I'm your guy!"
With a wink and a nod, oh my, so sly!
"Dance with the wind, let the laughter flow,
With every sip, we'll put on a show!"

Dancing with breezes, and playfully spun,
Quince does a twirl, "Isn't this fun?"
The elderberries giggle, slightly out of tune,
With laughter so bright, they brighten the moon!

As night settles down, crickets begin,
While apples chase stars, in a cheeky spin.
"Let's race for the clouds, over hills, through the glade,
We'll sing until morning, in this feast we've made!"

Colors of the Earthly Feast

In gardens vibrant, a palette unfolds,
Where veggies chuckle, with stories of old.
Eggplants boast in their velvety coats,
"You think you can beat me? Come on, take notes!"

Carrots dive deep, in playful disguise,
"I'm undercover, don't tell the wise!"
They wiggle and dance, from their cozy beds,
Sprouting up jokes, from their leafy heads!

Radishes pop, with a spicy jest,
"Let's spice up our lives, guys, it's the zest!"
Broccoli chortles, in its tree-like way,
"I've got the roots that are here to stay!"

With harvest moon shining, they all convene,
Pumpkins get cozy, shaping a scene.
"Time for a party, let's gather near!
With laughter and joy, spread the cheer!"

Whispers of Ripening Orchards

In orchards wide, the apples laugh,
They wiggle, jiggle, in their greenish gaff.
Cherries gossip with the breeze,
Telling tales of buzzing bees.

Peaches plump, they throw a dance,
Wobbling gently, they take a chance.
Lemons giggle, puckered tight,
Sour faces in pure delight.

Nectarines blush with golden glee,
Whispering softly, 'Come pick me!'
Underneath the sun's warm glow,
They chuckle in a playful row.

As shadows stretch and daylight fades,
The fruits keep up their silly charades.
With stems entwined and warning signs,
Saying, 'Stay back! We're sipping wines!'

Nectar's Embrace

In laughter's clutch, the berries twirl,
With every stomp, they spin and swirl.
A jester's crown upon their heads,
Strawberries joke while filling beds.

The oranges tease with zesty stems,
Blasting tunes from tiny gems.
While grapefruits smirk in yellow light,
Bartering giggles for a bite.

Pineapples wear their crowns so proud,
Sipping drinks and swaying loud.
Bananas chuckle, 'Look at us!'
Peeling laughter, no need to fuss.

As the harvest moon starts to peek,
The fruits unite, it's 'funny week!'
In nature's court, they feel so free,
Making merry in jubilee!

Gardens of Abundance

In gardens bright, the veggies prance,
Tomatoes tease with a saucy glance.
Carrots dig deep, hiding from sight,
While radishes ready for a late night.

Zucchini jiggles, making a scene,
"Mash us up and keep us keen!"
Cucumbers whisper fresh, cool tales,
While beans prepare their looping trails.

Sunflowers nod, their heads so high,
Winking at insects passing by.
They tell secrets, a blooming quest,
Of tasty bites – oh, what a fest!

As evening falls, the critters cheer,
With playful antics, no sign of fear.
In gardens lush, where laughter sows,
Nature's jesting surely grows!

Plum Blossoms in the Breeze

Plum blossoms twirl in a floral frolic,
While squirrels dance, their tails so symbolic.
In every petal, giggles unite,
Whispering secrets throughout the night.

Bees in tuxedos buzz with sass,
Having tea on the green blades of grass.
The plums declare, 'We're ripe and bold,
Don't dare leave us out in the cold!'

With every gust, the fruits take wing,
Swaying and swirling, they start to sing.
A symphony of flavor and fun,
In nature's theater, they all run.

As the moon glows and shadows reflect,
The fruits unite to laugh and connect.
In the breeze's arms, they twirl with ease,
Life's comedy among the trees!

Infused with Sunshine

Beneath a tree so round and bright,
Lemons laugh with pure delight.
They wear yellow hats, oh what a sight,
Sipping sunbeams, they feel just right.

A barrel of peaches, all in a cheer,
Giggle as they grow, year after year.
With fuzzy cheeks, they draw us near,
Warning, they may cause a fruit-filled tear!

Plums play games, roll down the hill,
With every splash, they shake up the chill.
In fruitball tournaments, they've got the skill,
Juicy and bold, they're always a thrill.

So let's raise a toast to this jolly lot,
With every bite, let's thank what we've got.
Every sweet giggle, every juicy thought,
In this orchard of laughter, we bloom like a spot.

The Whimsy of Nature's Palette

Carrots in capes, what a grand show,
Dancing around like they're in the know.
Broccoli bursts out in a funny row,
While cucumbers chill, taking it slow.

Raspberries giggle with their tiny crowns,
Wearing red dresses, twirling around.
Cherries parade, no frowns to be found,
Sweet-tasting laughter is what they compound.

Radishes joke, with a spicy surprise,
Laughing so hard, they roll like the pies.
Under the sun, where silliness lies,
Every new sprout is a feast for the eyes!

So gather them all, this whimsical crew,
Nature's jesters, each one's a clue.
To find all the joy in a colorful hue,
Let them tickle the senses; it's funny but true.

Roots and Fruits in Harmony

Down in the dirt, where the beetles cheer,
Radishes whisper, 'We're the root pioneers!'
While potatoes chuckle, gripping their spears,
'Hold on tight, let's take some beers!'

Up in the branches, the apples jest,
Dropping their jokes, they put strength to the test.
'We fall but we rise, we're simply the best!'
A bounce in their step, they forget all the rest.

Grapes in their clusters, they're giggling out loud,
Hanging on vines, feeling so proud.
With each little pop, they form a fun crowd,
Sipping sweet nectar, they're never too cowed.

So here's to the roots and fruits entwined,
In a world full of laughter, together aligned.
They teach us to savor, to seek and to find,
The joy of connection, so sweet and so kind.

A Dance of Color Against the Sky

Clouds above watch the peach parade,
As tangerines twirl in the grand charade.
Limes breakdance, they're never dismayed,
While banana boys strut, in yellow arrayed.

Mangoes stomp, flaunting their flair,
Creating a ruckus, without any care.
Kiwi kicks high, jumping through air,
While cherries burst forth, without any scare.

Berries unite for a boisterous soirée,
In berries and jams, all colors convey.
Laughing together, they dance and they play,
Painting the world in their own fruity way.

So while nature hums its hilarious song,
Join in the dance; you can't go wrong!
For in this color fiesta, the silliness throngs,
Life's sweetest moments will carry you along.

Lush Legacies of Life

In gardens rich with colors bright,
The gooseberries dance in the moonlight.
Cherries giggle in bubbles of dew,
Wearing jackets of vibrant hue.

Lemonades whisper secrets sweet,
With every sip, a tasty treat.
Bananas slide in a playful race,
While pineapples wear a spiky face.

The oranges do a salsa spin,
Twirling joy, laughter within.
Mangoes hide in a hammock's sway,
Ripe and ready for a sunny play.

Grapes jest around in a viney mess,
Joking about their juicy success.
With each bite, a chuckle is found,
In this fruity circus, joy abounds.

Whims of the Canopy

Up above where the sky's so wide,
Berries giggle as squirrels glide.
Coconuts tumble, a soft, loud thud,
While avocados ponder, 'What's up, bud?'

Pine nuts play peek-a-boo with the breeze,
Limes are laughing like they're at ease.
Kiwis bounce on their fuzzy toes,
Joking about their fuzzy woes.

Plum plops down with a plucky cheer,
Wishes on leaves, let's toast with a beer!
The fruit parade struts in vibrant hues,
Sharing tales of summer's views.

Pears play cards, all in a row,
While cherries count the stars in tow.
Bananas bring the jokes and glee,
In this tree-top party, all's fruity and free.

Eden's Bounty

In the orchard where giggles grow,
Peaches blush under the sun's glow.
Nuts snap jokes at the passing flies,
While the apples wear green disguise.

Tomatoes chuckle, red as a glow,
Mocking the squash, "You look like a pro!"
As cucumbers waddle in line so neat,
They jive and jolt, oh, what a feat!

Berries burst in a fruit cocktail,
Telling tales with a fruity unveil.
Pumpkins snicker, all plump and round,
While zesty citrus twirls all around.

In Eden's patch, where laughter runs free,
Each bite brings joy, like a fruit jubilee.
Harvest the smiles, don't let it stop,
In these gardens of giggles, we'll always hop!

Harvest Moon Melodies

Beneath the moon, the fruits sing loud,
Dancing in shadows, oh so proud.
Ripe figs strut with a jaunty flair,
While apples debate, 'Who's the fairest hair?'

Grapefruit jests with a tangy twist,
Claiming the spotlight, no chance to miss.
Raspberries chuckle, red and sweet,
With every burst, they can't be beat.

Under the stars, each fruit holds court,
Lemonade cheerleaders making the sport.
Watermelons roll, a playful sight,
In this carnival of flavors tonight.

With catchy tunes of berry delight,
They serenade the enchanting night.
So come, enjoy this festive spree,
Where laughter and fruits grow wild and free.

Singing Trees

In the garden, they sway and hum,
With floppy hats, they dance, oh so dumb.
Apple giggles, pear-shaped grins,
Lemon jokes make everyone spin.

Barking dogs join the leafy choir,
Barking tunes like a raucous fire.
Bananas split with laughter so bright,
While cherries roll in pure delight.

Coconut drums keep the beat alive,
As peachy punks start to jive.
All around, the silly sounds,
And the laughter grows in twists and bounds.

A Cornucopia of Dreams

In a basket where dreams collide,
Lemons whisper, "Come take a ride!"
Berries bounce with cheeky flair,
While grapes gossip without a care.

Radishes wear their jester hats,
Dancing round like playful brats.
Carrots joke, their tops in a knot,
"It's a veggie party, you're all forgot!"

Cabbages roll like big round balls,
They tumble and dive, on garden walls.
Each snack a tale, a fruity scheme,
Bite-size giggles, a dreamed-up theme!

Juicy Journeys

Take off with the fruity crew,
An orange car, bright and new.
Bananas driving, a silly sight,
Strawberry maps, guiding the flight.

Rolling down the hills with cheer,
Pineapples laugh as they steer.
Cherries shout, "Let's race and roll!"
Tomatoes squish, but that's their goal.

They journey through a candy land,
Sipping juice from a giant hand.
Clouds of whipped cream float so high,
Underneath the blueberry sky.

Laying Down in a Sea of Blossoms

In fields of blooms, we lay and dream,
Petals tickle, laughter streams.
Daisies giggle, a fragrant tease,
As bees debate who's got the cheese.

Buttercup hats crown silly heads,
Poppy jokes bounce on flower beds.
"Who borrowed my pollen?" a daffodil cries,
While sunflowers laugh, reaching for the skies.

A daisy chain, the perfect belt,
In this floral world, all worries melt.
Wander the rows, let whimsy lead,
In a sea of blossoms, we plant the seed.

Harvesting Memories in Vibrant Hues

In the orchard where laughter sings,
We pluck bright colors, oh what fun things!
Banana peels slip, giggles arise,
As oranges wiggle, much to our surprise.

The air is sweet; bees buzz with glee,
But watch out for that cheeky bee!
It almost stole my snack—how rude!
I guess it's just nature's blissful food.

Cherries dance on folks' big hats,
While squirrels plot with their sneaky chats.
"Just one more berry!"—oh what a pain,
Nature's buffet, but I'll complain.

We gather up colors, taste the dreams,
Slicing through giggles, spilling bright creams.
Every bite's a laugh, every cheer a kiss,
Harvesting joy in the fruity bliss.

A Cascade of Juices

Under the sun where the squishy stuff lands,
Watermelon giggles slip through our hands.
We dive in like fish, fruity drips on our face,
Turns out juice fights aren't a graceful chase!

Pineapple crowns laugh atop our heads,
While ripe avocados lounge in their beds.
"Is that a smoothie or rain from the trees?"
"A juice disaster!"—we're buzzing with ease.

Carrots in shorts, looking quite sleek,
Dance with the peas, they have cheeky beaks.
"Can we juice this salad?" we ask with a grin,
But it squirts back, "You've all lost your spin!"

The blender hums out tunes of delight,
As we mix and shake till it's out of sight.
A cascade of flavors, splashes galore,
At the juice party, who could ask for more?

The Heartbeat of Blossoming Fields

In fields where giggles and wiggles unite,
The veggies are gossiping, such a delight!
Tomatoes red in their plump little spots,
Laughing at carrots tied up in knots.

Cucumbers waltz, in a leafy ballet,
While sprouts begin schemes in a leafy fray.
"Who's the best dancer?"—they argue with pride,
But pumpkin just rolls, he don't need to hide!

The sun spills its laughter on rows of green dreams,
With whispers from onions in mischievous schemes.
Every crunch is a joke, every bite a burst,
In this quirky realm, there's joy—we're immersed!

So let's dance in the soil, twirl till we drop,
In this heartbeat of life, we'll never stop.
With each wave of the plants, our spirits will swell,
In these blossoming fields, there's fun to dispel!

Sweetness Underfoot

Underfoot, a treasure trove of delight,
The sweet crumbs of snacks make the ants take flight.
Bananas peel back giggles and slips,
As pies sneak away on mischievous trips.

Strawberries pop up like surprise little pals,
Dancing with grapes in their vibrant thralls.
"Watch your step!" shouts the old apple tree,
But we're wading through sweetness, wild and free!

Cobbler crumbs scatter with a cheeky flair,
While jellybeans tumble from skyward air.
We tumble and slip, it's chaotic and fun,
In the sweetness below, we race—never done!

Every step is a giggle, a bounce, a cheer,
With laughter as rich as the fruits we revere.
So relish the mess, embrace every squish,
In the land where sweetness lives, there's no wish!

Fragrant Promises Unfold

In the orchard, there's a show,
With fruits dancing in a row.
They wiggle and they twist with glee,
As squirrels cheer on from a tree.

Bananas wear their peels so bright,
Telling jokes that spark delight.
While cherries giggle, round and bold,
Their laughter makes the sunshine gold.

Oranges roll, they slip and slide,
A citrus party, full of pride.
Lemons squeeze out every pun,
In this grove of joy and fun!

So come along, let's skip and sing,
Join the fruity, joyful fling.
In this land, the laughter flows,
Unfolding joy as color grows.

Enchantment in Every Bite

A pear once whispered, "Take a bite,"
And I fell over in delight.
Mangoes wore their skirts so high,
I think they're flaunting, oh my my!

Berries beamed in shades so bright,
Telling tales of sweet delight.
Each munch a giggle, each chew a cheer,
With every slice, the jokes come near.

Pineapples stand in regal pose,
Crowning laughter like a rose.
They crack a joke, you'll see them shine,
In the banquet of this fruity line.

So feast your eyes, indulge your whims,
With every bite, the joy just swims.
In a world where laughter's tight,
Enjoy the groove, it's pure delight!

Delicate Dreams of the Grove

In the grove, a peach took flight,
Dreaming dreams of pure delight.
Grapes all twinkled, dressed in dew,
Spinning tales that felt brand new.

A merry melon hopped with flair,
As kiwi spun like it just don't care.
"Catch me if you can!" it yelled,
While puzzled pumpkins just spelled.

Under the sun, they play and sway,
With silly games that last all day.
Their giggles softly fill the air,
As dancing fruits, they're quite the pair!

So if you hear that joyful sound,
Join the fun, let laughter abound.
In this grove, let dreams take flight,
Where every twist brings pure delight.

Nectar of the Wild

Down in the wild, the fruits unite,
Sprouting jokes, oh what a sight!
Berries whisper silly rhymes,
Laughing softly through the times.

A grapefruit with its zany grin,
Said, "Juice your worries, let fun begin!"
Avocados played a game of tag,
While nuts forgot their little brag.

Coconuts fell with a funny plop,
Each plinky plink made giggles pop.
They splashed and played in sunshine's ray,
In this wild world, let's laugh all day!

So grab a seat on this fruity ride,
And let the giggles be your guide.
With every taste, the joy's instilled,
In the nectar of the wild, be thrilled!

www.ingramcontent.com/pod-product-compliance
Lightning Source LLC
Chambersburg PA
CBHW060127230426
43661CB00003B/357